Usborne
Guitar
for beginners

Minna Lacey

Designed by Laura Hammonds
Illustrated by Candice Whatmore and Lizzie Barber

Edited by Sam Taplin
Guitar adviser: Patrick Hatchett
Music consultant: Anthony Marks

With thanks to Catherine Duffy and Andrew Jones

Contents

About this book

The guitar is a wonderful instrument to learn. You can play
it in lots of different ways and adapt it to almost any style of
music, from folk, pop and rock to jazz and classical.
It sounds impressive as a solo instrument and is one of
the most popular instruments for accompanying songs
and playing with others in a group.

This is a step-by-step introduction to playing the guitar for
beginners of any age. It includes lots of songs to play, with
clear instructions and diagrams to show you what to do.
This book will tell you everything a beginner needs to
know, from how to hold the instrument, and which kind
of guitar to choose, to how to pluck and strum the strings.
After mastering a few techniques, beginners can quickly
learn how to play simple melodies, strum chords and
find out the basics of how to read music.

Internet links

If you have a computer, you can listen to all the tunes in this book on the Usborne
Quicklinks Website to hear how they go. You can also try playing along in time to
the music on the recordings. Just go to **www.usborne-quicklinks.com** and type
in the keywords "Guitar for beginners", then follow the simple instructions.

Different kinds of guitars

There are three main types of guitars: classical, electric and steel-string. Classical and steel-string guitars are both acoustic guitars, which means they create a sound using the strings and the body of the guitar. Electric guitars need to be plugged into an extra piece of equipment called an amplifier, to be loud enough to hear well.

Classical guitars

A classical guitar, also known as a Spanish guitar, has a hollow body and a wide fingerboard. The strings are made of nylon, with the three lowest sounding strings wound with metal.

This kind of guitar creates a warm, mellow tone and can be used for almost any musical style, except for loud rock and heavy metal music.

Head

Neck

Tuning pegs

Nut

Fingerboard

Frets

Body

Sound hole

6th string

1st string

Saddle

Bridge

Many beginners find it easier to start learning on a classical guitar.

5

Steel-string guitars

A steel-string guitar, also known as a folk guitar, usually has a narrower fingerboard than a classical guitar, and makes a stronger, harder sound. It often has a wider lower part of the body and a metal rod within the neck to support the steel strings. This kind of guitar is often used for blues, country and folk music.

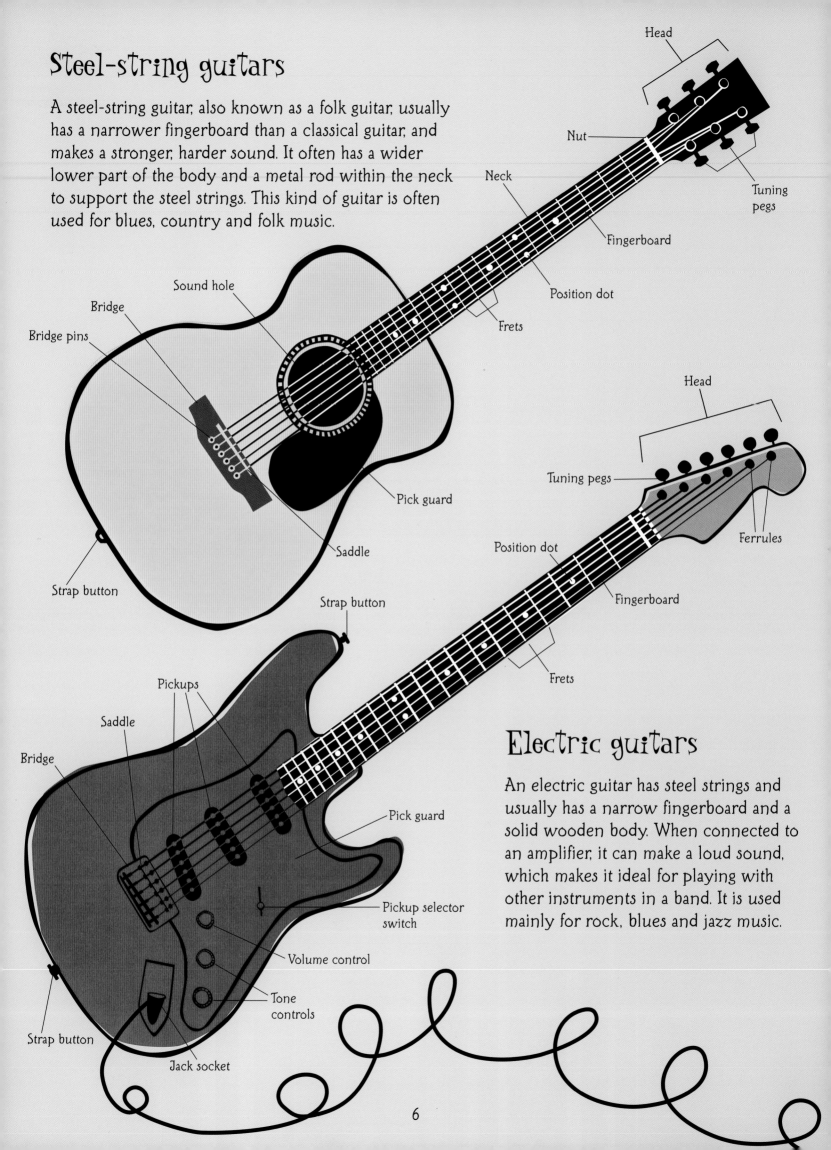

Head

Nut

Neck

Tuning pegs

Fingerboard

Position dot

Frets

Sound hole

Bridge

Bridge pins

Pick guard

Saddle

Strap button

Head

Tuning pegs

Ferrules

Position dot

Fingerboard

Frets

Strap button

Pickups

Saddle

Bridge

Pick guard

Pickup selector switch

Volume control

Tone controls

Strap button

Jack socket

Electric guitars

An electric guitar has steel strings and usually has a narrow fingerboard and a solid wooden body. When connected to an amplifier, it can make a loud sound, which makes it ideal for playing with other instruments in a band. It is used mainly for rock, blues and jazz music.

Choosing a guitar

A classical guitar is probably the best type of guitar for beginners to learn on. Its nylon strings are softer to press on than steel strings, which means your fingers won't get so sore when you start playing. It can also be played anywhere. Electric guitars are fun to play but they are heavier than classical guitars and need to be played near an electric socket.

Tips for buying a guitar

It's important to find a guitar that is the right size for you. Young children will find it easier to start off with a half-size or three-quarter-size guitar.

Make sure the tuning pegs are easy to turn.

Make sure the neck doesn't curve or twist in any direction.

It's important that the bridge and saddle are fixed securely.

Pluck and strum the strings for a few minutes to make sure they ring clearly.

If you're not sure, ask someone you know who plays the guitar to come along with you to help you choose.

Taking care of your guitar

Always wash your hands before playing. The guitar will not sound as good if the strings are dirty.

After playing, it's a good idea to wipe the wood and strings gently with a soft dry cloth to remove dust and grease.

Put your guitar away in its case when you have finished cleaning it. Don't leave it near a radiator or in direct sunlight.

How to hold your guitar

The usual way to hold a guitar is to support the neck in your left hand, while your right hand plucks the strings. Most left- and right-handed players hold the guitar in this way. A few people, however, may find it easier to play a left-handed guitar that you hold the other way around.

If you play a left-handed guitar, you will need to reverse the instructions for the left and right hand in this book.

Many guitarists like to sit cross-legged, with their right leg over their left.

Classical guitarists often sit with their left leg slightly raised on a foot stool.

You can also play standing up, if you have a strap attached to strap buttons on your guitar*.

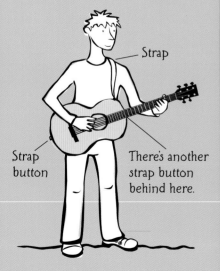

Strap

Strap button

There's another strap button behind here.

*If you don't have strap buttons, then you can ask at a store to have them added on.

Sit up straight with your shoulders relaxed, not hunched up.

Lean forward a little.

Let the guitar lean gently against your chest.

Tilt the neck of the guitar slightly upward.

Rest your right forearm on the widest part of the guitar.

Balance your weight evenly.

Use a chair without armrests.

Feeling comfortable

When practicing the guitar, it's best to find a position that feels really comfortable. Holding the guitar correctly will give you better control over your fingers and prevent you from feeling tension in your body, which can make you feel sore or achy. When you start off, it's best not to play for too long at once. If you feel any aches or pains, you should stop playing and take a rest.

Making music

Music is made up of sounds called notes. On the guitar, you can make notes by plucking the strings with your right hand, and by pressing the strings on the fingerboard with your left hand. You press the strings between metal bars, called frets.

Notes

Notes range from very low sounds to very high sounds. They are named after the first seven letters of the alphabet: A, B, C, D, E, F, G. This sequence repeats itself again and again as the notes get higher or lower. Once you know a few notes on the guitar, you can play a tune.

Strings

Most guitars have six strings: high E, B, G, D, A and low E. High E is also called the 1st string, and is closest to the floor when you hold the guitar. Low E is also called the 6th string and is closest to your face when you hold the guitar.

When you pluck a string without pressing it down on the fingerboard, it is called an "open string." You can try plucking the six open strings in turn.

Frets

Frets are raised metal bars that cross the fingerboard. They are numbered 1, 2, 3 and so on, from the nut.

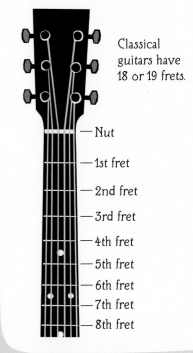

Classical guitars have 18 or 19 frets.

— Nut
— 1st fret
— 2nd fret
— 3rd fret
— 4th fret
— 5th fret
— 6th fret
— 7th fret
— 8th fret

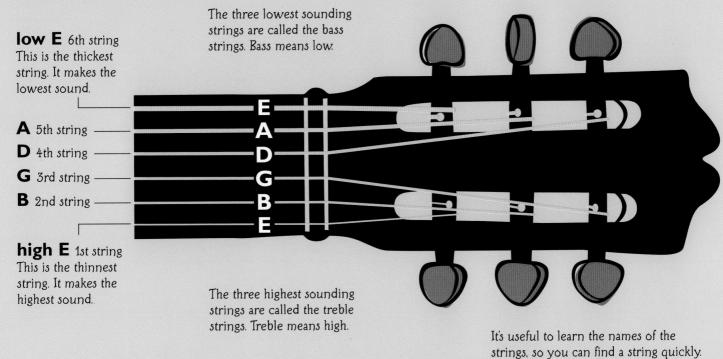

low E 6th string
This is the thickest string. It makes the lowest sound.

A 5th string
D 4th string
G 3rd string
B 2nd string

high E 1st string
This is the thinnest string. It makes the highest sound.

The three lowest sounding strings are called the bass strings. Bass means low.

The three highest sounding strings are called the treble strings. Treble means high.

It's useful to learn the names of the strings, so you can find a string quickly. Eventually you'll be able to do this without thinking about it.

Tuners

Pitchpipes

Blow the pipe marked low E and pluck low E on the guitar. Adjust the string with the tuning peg until it sounds the same as the pipe. Continue with each pipe and string in turn.

Electronic tuner

Turn on the electronic tuner and pluck low E. Tighten or loosen the string until the tuner shows it is in tune. Often a green light will appear when the string is at the correct pitch. Do the same with each string in turn.

Piano or keyboard

Play the second E below middle C on the piano and tune low E to this. You can see which notes to press in the picture below. Continue with each note in turn.

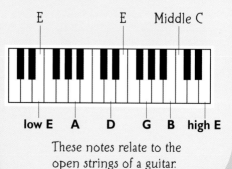

These notes relate to the open strings of a guitar.

Tuning your guitar

The 'pitch' is how high or low a string sounds. Before you start playing, you need to check that all the strings on your guitar are at the correct pitch. To change the pitch of the strings, you need to turn the pegs at the top of the guitar. This is called "tuning." Tuning can be hard to do at first, but it becomes much easier with practice.

To help you know whether each string is at the right pitch, you need to use a tuner, like the ones illustrated on this page. With most tuners, you need to pluck a string, listen to it, then see if it matches the tuner.

To make a string sound higher, tighten the string by turning the tuning peg away from you.

Use very small turns. If you tighten a string too much, it may snap.

To make a string sound lower, loosen the string by turning the peg toward you.

Tip

If you don't have a tuner, you can use a method called the "5th fret trick" to tune the guitar to itself. You can find out how to do this on page 60.

Open string accompaniments

How to pluck the strings

To pluck the strings, you can use your right-hand fingers and thumb, or a triangular piece of plastic called a plectrum, or pick. The best place to pluck the strings is directly over the sound hole. To begin with, it's best to get used to playing with your fingers and thumb, rather than a plectrum, especially on a classical guitar.

Using a plectrum

Some guitarists prefer to pluck the strings with a plectrum, or pick. This creates a stronger, brighter sound. It's common to use a plectrum with an electric guitar.

Hold the plectrum firmly between your thumb and index finger. Pluck the string with the tip of the plectrum. Strike downward – toward your knee – for a downstroke, and upward – toward your face – for an upstroke.

There are many different types of plectrums. Some are light and bendy, while others are stiff. It's best to start off with a thin or medium thickness.

Finger names

The most common plucking fingers are the "index" and "middle" fingers.

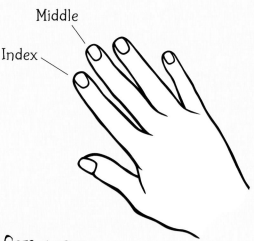

Middle

Index

Plucking with your fingers

Rest the tip of your index or middle finger on one of the treble strings, over the sound hole. Your finger should be curved a little. Press down and across the string, letting your finger come to rest on the next string. This is called "rest stroke."

As you pluck the string with your fingers, rest your thumb gently on the 6th string.

Keep your finger close to the guitar. Don't let your finger straighten out.

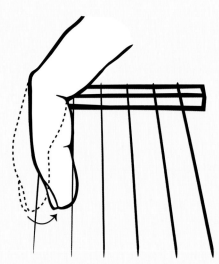

The plucking movement should just be in your fingers, while the rest of your hand stays still.

Plucking warm-up

It's a good idea to warm up with a few simple exercises, like these, every time you practice. This will strengthen your fingers and help you play more smoothly.

Note diagrams

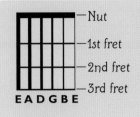

You will find note diagrams like this throughout the book. In the diagram the nut is at the top, the horizontal lines are the frets and the vertical lines are strings. The string to play is marked in red.

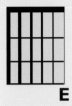

E E E E

Pluck high E, the 1st string, four times with your middle finger.

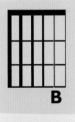

B B B B

Pluck B, the 2nd string, four times with your index finger.

E B E B E B E B

Now alternate between high E with your middle finger and B with your index finger. Make the change between notes as smooth as possible.

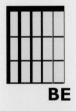

B B B B

Pluck B four times with your middle finger.

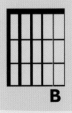

G G G G

Pluck G, the 3rd string, four times with your index finger.

B G B G B G B G

Now alternate between B with your middle finger and G with your index finger.

Walking fingers

To get the right plucking movement when you alternate between the index and middle fingers, it helps to imagine that you are taking your fingers for a walk.

Pease pudding hot

You are now ready to play an accompaniment on three strings. An accompaniment is when you play along to the music, rather than playing the melody, or tune. After practicing it a few times, you can listen to the tune and the accompaniment on the Usborne Quicklinks Website and try playing along*.

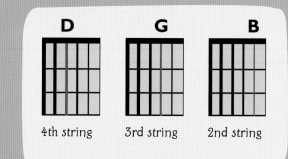

D	G	B
4th string	3rd string	2nd string

Beats

Music is measured in steady counts, called beats. You can feel a regular beat or pulse continuing throughout most music. In this song, the beats are counted in fours. Pluck the string at the beginning of each count of four.

The name of the string to play is written above the point in the words where you must pluck the string.

Pluck G with your index finger, then alternate between your index and middle fingers throughout the music.

Bars

To help you read the music, it is divided into sections called bars, marked by vertical bar-lines. Each bar has the same number of beats.

Bar-line

Bar

1 2 3 4 | 1 2 3 4 | 1 2 3 4 |

Beats

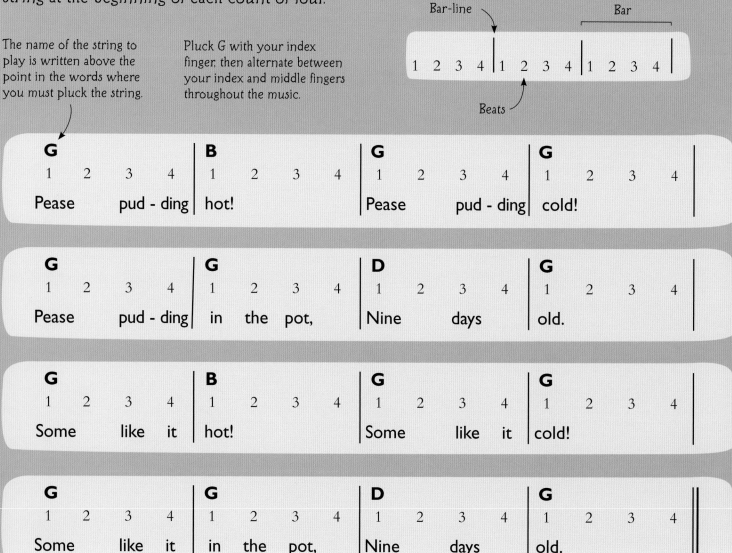

G
1   2   3   4
Pease   pud - ding

B
1   2   3   4
hot!

G
1   2   3   4
Pease   pud - ding

G
1   2   3   4
cold!

G
1   2   3   4
Pease   pud - ding

G
1   2   3   4
in   the   pot,

D
1   2   3   4
Nine   days

G
1   2   3   4
old.

G
1   2   3   4
Some   like   it

B
1   2   3   4
hot!

G
1   2   3   4
Some   like   it

G
1   2   3   4
cold!

G
1   2   3   4
Some   like   it

G
1   2   3   4
in   the   pot,

D
1   2   3   4
Nine   days

G
1   2   3   4
old.

* To find the Usborne Quicklinks Website, go to **www.usborne-quicklinks.com** and type in the keywords "Guitar for beginners", then follow the simple instructions.

Are you sleeping?

This song is an English translation of the French song Frère Jacques. Before you start the accompaniment, try counting the beats and clapping the rhythm below. This will help you get ready to play on every second beat.

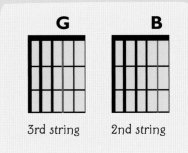

G   B

3rd string   2nd string

A clap is marked by a ↓

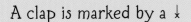

Clap	↓		↓		↓		↓		↓		↓		↓		↓	
Count	1	2	3	4	1	2	3	4	1	2	3	4	1	2	3	4

To play along to this song, you need to pluck G with your index finger and B with your middle finger on every second beat. Practice doing this a few times. When you feel ready, you can try playing along with the music on the Usborne Quicklinks Website.

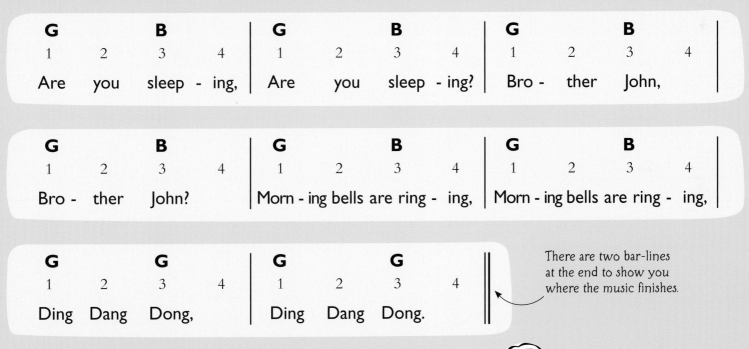

G		**B**		**G**		**B**		**G**		**B**	
1	2	3	4	1	2	3	4	1	2	3	4
Are	you	sleep - ing,		Are	you	sleep - ing?		Bro -	ther	John,	

G		**B**		**G**		**B**		**G**		**B**	
1	2	3	4	1	2	3	4	1	2	3	4
Bro -	ther	John?		Morn - ing bells are ring - ing,				Morn - ing bells are ring - ing,			

G		**G**		**G**		**G**	
1	2	3	4	1	2	3	4
Ding	Dang	Dong,		Ding	Dang	Dong.	

There are two bar-lines at the end to show you where the music finishes.

Playing in time

It doesn't matter how slowly you play the notes, as long as you try to play in time. This means keeping a steady beat throughout the music. It helps to count the beats in your head or tap your foot as you go along.

Try tapping your foot on every beat to help you play in time.

London's burning

This song has three beats in every bar. Before you start playing, try counting the beats and clapping the rhythm below. This will help you get used to playing on every beat.

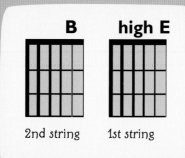

A clap is marked by a ⨡

Clap	⨡	⨡	⨡	⨡	⨡	⨡	⨡	⨡	⨡	⨡	⨡	⨡
Count	1	2	3	1	2	3	1	2	3	1	2	3

Play high E, where E is marked in the music. Pluck high E with your middle finger and B with your index finger. You can count the beats in threes as you go along.

	E	E	B	E	E	B
	1	2	3	1	2	3
London's	burn -	ing,	London's	burn -	ing,	Fetch the

E	E	B	E	E	E
1	2	3	1	2	3
en -	gines,	Fetch the	en -	gines,	Fire!

E	E	E	E	E	B
1	2	3	1	2	3
Fire!		Fire!	Fire!		Pour on

E	E	B	E	E	
1	2	3	1	2	3
wa -	ter,	Pour on	wa -	ter.	

Muffled notes

If any notes sound muffled when you play them, check the position of your plucking hand and try again. Make sure that none of your other fingers is touching the string you are plucking, as this could make it sound dull.

Alternating fingers

In the "Fire! Fire!" section of this song, try plucking the high E string alternately with your index and middle finger.

Plucking with your thumb

You use your thumb mostly to pluck the bass strings – low E, A and D. Rest your thumb on the string to be played. Stroke across the string, moving your thumb downward and forward so that it ends above the next string. This is called "free stroke."

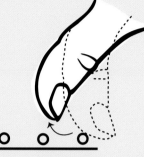

Rest your fingers lightly on the treble strings as you pluck with your thumb. Keep your thumb straight, but relaxed, as you play.

Rest stroke

You can make a stronger sound with your thumb by using a "rest" stroke. Rest your thumb on the string, then stroke down across the string, letting your thumb come to rest on the next string.

Let your thumb fall freely to the next string in a relaxed movement.

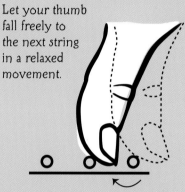

A rest stroke is useful when playing slowly. When playing faster, however, it is easier to use the free stroke.

You can practice doing the thumb exercises on this page using the rest stroke or the free stroke.

Warm-up exercises

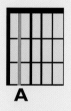

E

E E E E

Pluck low E four times with your thumb.

A

A A A A

Pluck A four times with your thumb.

EA

E A E A E A E A

Alternate plucking between low E and A. Make the change between notes as smooth as possible.

D

D D D D

Pluck D four times with your thumb.

AD

A D A D A D A D

Alternate plucking between A and D.

Skip to my Lou

In this song, pluck the bass strings low E and A with your thumb at the beginning of each bar. Play the notes slowly at first. When you are ready, you can listen to the recording on the Usborne Quicklinks Website and play along to the music.

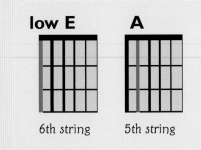

low E   **A**

6th string   5th string

Play low E where E is marked in the music.

A					A				
1	2	3	4		1	2	3	4	
Lost	my	part	-	ner,	What	shall	I	do?	

E					E				
1	2	3	4		1	2	3	4	
Lost	my	part	-	ner,	What	shall	I	do?	

A					A				
1	2	3	4		1	2	3	4	
Lost	my	part	-	ner,	What	shall	I	do?	

E					A				
1	2	3	4		1	2	3	4	
Skip	to	my	Lou	my	dar_____		ling._____		

Keeping a steady beat

Try not to pause when you change to a different string. You should try to keep playing in time, on the first beat of each bar. Remember to keep a steady beat, or pulse, throughout the music.

Resting fingers

Make sure your right-hand fingers are relaxed when you pluck the bass strings with your thumb. Your fingers should be slightly curved, with the fingertips resting on the treble strings.

Michael Finnegan

For this song you need to pluck the bass strings A and D with your thumb. Pluck once at the beginning of each bar. As you pluck the strings, make sure only your thumb moves, and not your whole hand.

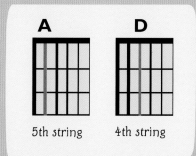

A   D

5th string   4th string

D				**D**			
1	2	3	4	1	2	3	4
There was	an old	man	called	Mi - chael		Fin - ne - gan,	

A				**A**			
1	2	3	4	1	2	3	4
He	grew	whis -	kers	on	his	chin - ne - gan, The	

D				**D**			
1	2	3	4	1	2	3	4
wind	came	out	and	blew	them	in - a -	gain,

A				**D**			
1	2	3	4	1	2	3	4
Poor	old	Mi -	chael	Fin - ne - gan	be - gin	a - gain!	

Practice makes perfect

Try to practice for at least ten minutes a day. It helps to do it at roughly the same time each day, so that it becomes part of a routine. You will improve much more quickly if you practice a little and often than if you play for a long time once every two weeks.

Swing low, sweet chariot

This song has four beats in each bar. You need to play the bass strings A and D with your thumb, plucking on every beat. When you have finished, you could try the whole accompaniment again using the bass strings A and low E instead, starting on the A string.

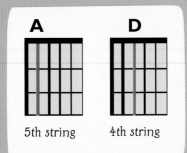

A	D
5th string	4th string

D	D	D	D	D	D	A	A
1	2	3	4	1	2	3	4
Swing	low,_____		sweet	cha_____		ri - ot._____	

D	D	D	D	A	A	A	A
1	2	3	4	1	2	3	4
Com - ing	for	to	car - ry	me	home._____		

D	D	D	D	D	D	A	A
1	2	3	4	1	2	3	4
Swing	low,_____		sweet	cha_____		ri - ot._____	

D	D	A	A	D	D	D	D
1	2	3	4	1	2	3	4
Com - ing	for	to	car - ry	me	home._____		

Play gently

When you are practicing, try not to pluck the strings too hard – or the notes will sound too loud and twangy. You can make a clearer and more even sound by playing gently.

Using the fingerboard

Musical steps

The distance between notes in music is measured in steps, called tones, and half-steps, called semitones.

The distance between one fret and the next on a guitar is a semitone. A tone is the distance between any two frets.

Fretting finger

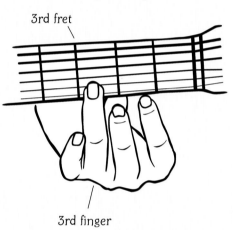

As a general rule, use your 1st finger to fret the 1st fret, the 2nd finger to fret the 2nd fret and the 3rd finger to fret the 3rd fret.

Fingernails

It's a good idea to keep your left-hand fingernails short. This makes it easier to fret the strings.

The left hand

Your left hand is used to press down on the strings by the frets. When you press on a string, you shorten the vibrating part of the string, which makes it sound higher.

Left-hand fingers

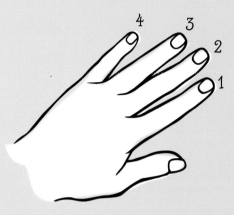

The left-hand fingers are numbered from 1 to 4. You will see these numbers in note diagrams to show you which left-hand fingers to use.

Thumb position

Keep your thumb straight and your elbow tucked in. Don't grip too hard.

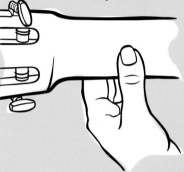

Place your thumb on the back of the neck, opposite your first finger. Keep your thumb low on the neck, so your fingers can reach further on the fingerboard.

Fretting position

Try to keep a space between your hand and the guitar.

With your thumb behind the neck, place the tip of your fretting finger just to the left of the fret as you hold the guitar (to the right in this picture).

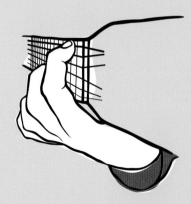

Your fretting finger should arch over the fingerboard so that only the tip rests on the string. Press firmly on the string to make a clear sound.

Go tell Aunt Nancy

To play the accompaniment to this song, you need to learn a new note, A, on the 3rd string. To play this note, press your 2nd finger on the 3rd string, by the 2nd fret.

Note lengths

Notes last for different lengths of time. Learning how long or short different kinds of notes are will help you understand the rhythm of the music.

o   This note is called a whole note. It lasts for four beats.

Pluck the strings with your index and middle fingers on the 1st beat of each bar, like this.

o			
1	2	3	4

Notes used

In these note diagrams, the white dot shows you where to press on the string, which is marked in red. The number shows you which left-hand finger to use.

G
3rd string
Open

A
3rd string
2nd fret

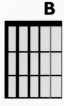
B
2nd string
Open

Tip

When you see a whole note o in the music, count "one, two, three, four."

B				**G**				**A**			
o				o				o			
1	2	3	4	1	2	3	4	1	2	3	4
Go_____		tell	Aunt	Nan	-		cy,	Go_____		tell	Aunt

G				**B**				**B**			
o				o				o			
1	2	3	4	1	2	3	4	1	2	3	4
Nan	-		cy.	Go_____		tell	Aunt	Nan	-	cy	the

A				**G**			
o				o			
1	2	3	4	1	2	3	4
old	grey	goose	is	dead._____			

Bobby Shafto

Before you start, practice the following note sequence G B G D A D G G until you can play it smoothly.

Note lengths

♩ This note is called a quarter note. It lasts for one beat.

Play the guitar accompaniment on each beat, like this:

♩	♩	♩	♩
1	2	3	4

Notes used

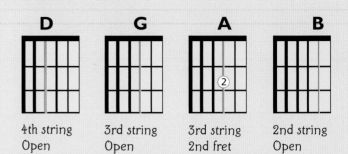

D	G	A	B
4th string Open	3rd string Open	3rd string 2nd fret	2nd string Open

Buzzing notes

If a string makes a buzz when you press on it, try pressing a little harder on the string and moving your finger closer to the fret – but not on top of the fret. Keep adjusting your finger until the buzzing stops.

G	G	B	G		D	D	D	D
♩	♩	♩	♩		♩	♩	♩	♩
1	2	3	4		1	2	3	4
Bob - by	Shaf - to's	gone	to	sea,	Sil - ver	bu - ckles	on	his	knee,

G	G	B	G		A	D	G	G
♩	♩	♩	♩		♩	♩	♩	♩
1	2	3	4		1	2	3	4
He'll come	home and	mar - ry	me,	Bon - nie	Bob - by	Shaf	- to

B	B	B	B		A	A	A	A
♩	♩	♩	♩		♩	♩	♩	♩
1	2	3	4		1	2	3	4
Bob - by	Shaf - to's	fat	and	fair,	Comb - ing	down his	yel - low	hair;

B	B	B	B		A	D	G	G
♩	♩	♩	♩		♩	♩	♩	♩
1	2	3	4		1	2	3	4
He's my	love for	ev - er -	more,	Bon - nie	Bob - by	Shaf	- to.

London Bridge is falling down

To play D on the 2nd string, press your 3rd finger on the 2nd string by the 3rd fret.

Note lengths

This is a half note. It lasts for two quarter beats.

Play the accompaniment on the 1st and 3rd beats in each bar, like this:

1   2   3   4

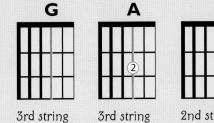

Notes used

G	A	B	D
3rd string Open	3rd string 2nd fret	2nd string Open	2nd string 3rd fret

Tip

When you see a half note ♩, count "one, two."

D   **B**   **A**   **B**

1   2   3   4   1   2   3   4

Lon - don   Bridge   is   fall - ing   down,_____

D   **B**   **A**   **G**

1   2   3   4   1   2   3   4

Fall - ing   down,_____   Fall - ing   down,_____

D   **B**   **A**   **B**

1   2   3   4   1   2   3   4

Lon - don   Bridge   is   fall - ing   down,_____

D   **B**   **A**   **G**

1   2   3   4   1   2   3   4

My   fair   la - dy._____

25

Scarborough Fair

Note lengths

♩. This note is called a "dotted half note." A note with a dot after it lasts half as long again. So a dotted half note lasts for a half note and a quarter note together.

A half note + a quarter note = 3 quarter notes.

In the music below, there is one dotted half note in each bar. You need to play the accompaniment on the 1st beat in each bar.

♩.		
1	2	3

Notes used

G	A	C	D
3rd string Open	3rd string 2nd fret	2nd string 1st fret	2nd string 3rd fret

Tip

When you see a dotted half note ♩. , count "one, two, three."

G	**D**	**A**	**G**
♩.	♩.	♩.	♩.
1 2 3	1 2 3	1 2 3	1 2 3
Are you	going to	Scar - bor - ough	Fair?_____

G	**G**	**D**	**D**	**G**
♩.	♩.	♩.	♩.	♩.
1 2 3	1 2 3	1 2 3	1 2 3	1 2 3
Par - sley,	sage, rose	-ma - ry and	thyme._____	Re -

G	**D**	**D**	**C**	**D**
♩.	♩.	♩.	♩.	♩.
1 2 3	1 2 3	1 2 3	1 2 3	1 2 3
mem - ber	me to	one who lives	there,_____	

G	**C**	**D**	**G**	**G**
♩.	♩.	♩.	♩.	♩.
1 2 3	1 2 3	1 2 3	1 2 3	1 2 3
She once	was a	true love of	mine._____	

26

Land of the silver birch

Note lengths

♪ This note is called an eighth note. It looks like a quarter note with a tail and lasts for half as long. Two eighth notes last for one quarter note.

♫ Two eighth notes in a row are joined together, like this. You can see pairs of eighth notes in the music below.

Try clapping this rhythm before you start playing:

1	2 - and	3	4	tea	cof- fee	tea	tea

To learn this rhythm, it helps to make up some words to go with it, like this.

Notes used

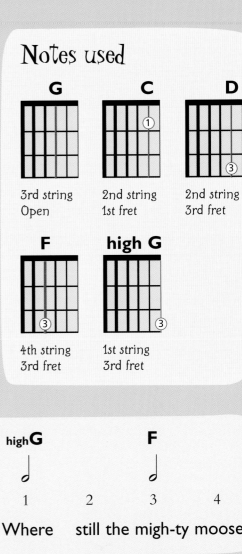

G — 3rd string Open
C — 2nd string 1st fret
D — 2nd string 3rd fret
F — 4th string 3rd fret
high G — 1st string 3rd fret

G	G	G	D	D	G	G	G	D	D	high G		F	
1	2		3	4	1	2		3	4	1	2	3	4
Land	of	the	sil-ver	birch,	Home	of	the	bea -	ver,	Where	still the	migh-ty	moose

C		D		high G		F		C		D	
1	2	3	4	1	2	3	4	1	2	3	4
Wan - ders at	will._____			Blue	lake and rock-y	shore,		I		will re - turn once more.	

G	G	G	G	G	G	G	G	G	G	G	G	G	G
1	2		3	4	1	2		3	4	1	2		3	4
Boom	di-ddy	boom	boom	Boom	di-ddy	boom	boom	Boom	di-ddy	boom	boom

G			
1	2	3	4
boom._____			

Note lengths

When you play the guitar, it's important to understand the rhythm of the music. This means learning how long or short different kinds of note are. If you can remember the note lengths you have just been learning about, it will help you learn how to read music more quickly and master the right rhythm of new songs and tunes.

Rests

Sometimes there is a silence in the middle of the music. This is called a rest. Rests, like notes, last for different amounts of time, and have different symbols to identify them.

♩ This is a quarter note rest. It lasts for one quarter note.

When you see a ♩ in the music, place your finger on the string you have just played to stop it from ringing, then rest for one quarter note beat.

▬ This is a half note rest. It lasts for one half note or two quarter note beats.

When you see a ▬ , rest for two quarter note beats.

Try plucking these rhythms on the guitar, on any string.

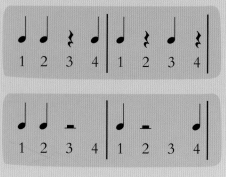

𝅝		Whole note	4 beats
𝅗𝅥.		Dotted half note	3 beats
𝅗𝅥		Half note	2 beats
♩		Quarter note	1 beat
♪		Eighth note	1/2 beat

Try clapping the following rhythms. Then pluck them on the guitar, on any string.

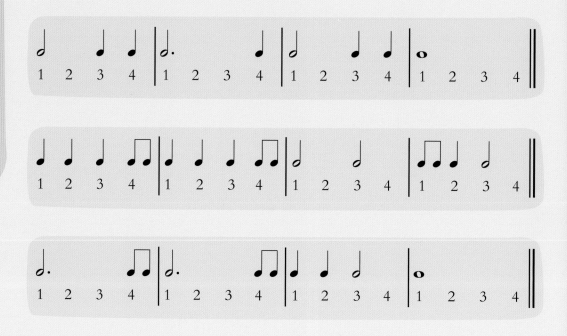

Playing the melody

How to read music

Reading music is important for learning how to play new tunes. Some guitar music uses traditional music symbols, while some uses a system called tablature, or tab. Many guitarists use both systems.

Traditional music symbols

Music can be written in notes on a set of lines, called a staff, or stave.

At the beginning of the staff is a sign called a treble clef.

Some notes are written on the lines of the stave. Other notes are written in the spaces between the lines. The higher a note is placed on the staff, the higher its pitch.

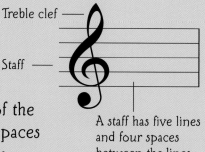

Treble clef —

Staff —

A staff has five lines and four spaces between the lines.

Time signatures

After the treble clef sign are two numbers, called the time signature. This tells you how many beats there are in each bar.

The top number tells you the number of beats in one complete bar.

The bottom number tells you the type of beat. A "4" means a quarter note beat.

This is what the bottom numbers of the time signature mean.

2 – half note
4 – quarter note
8 – eighth note

$\frac{4}{4}$ } 4 quarter note beats in a bar.

$\frac{3}{4}$ } 3 quarter note beats in a bar.

$\frac{2}{4}$ } 2 quarter note beats in a bar.

$\frac{6}{8}$ } 6 eighth note beats in a bar.

Notes on lines

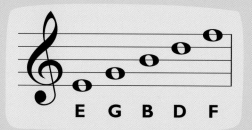

E G B D F

You can remember the notes on the lines by learning the following phrase:

Every **G**ood **B**oy **D**eserves **F**ootball

Notes in spaces

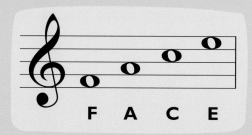

F A C E

You can remember the notes in the spaces by spelling out the word:

F A C E ("FACE" rhymes with space.)

Notes with sharps and flats

♯ This is a sharp sign.

A ♯ in front of a note makes it higher by a half step, or semitone. This means you play the note one fret higher.

♭ This is a flat sign.

A ♭ in front of a note makes it lower by a half step, or semitone. This means you play the note one fret lower.

Tablature

A tablature (or tab) chart is a different way of reading guitar music. It has six horizontal lines, that represent the strings of the guitar. The top line is high E, the 1st string, and the bottom line is low E, the 6th string. The numbers on the lines show which fret is to be used.

In the chart, 0 means play an open string, 1 means press down by the 1st fret and 2 means press down by the 2nd fret.

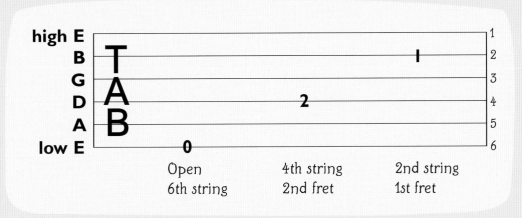

Open
6th string

4th string
2nd fret

2nd string
1st fret

See if you can follow the tab below, then try to play it through very slowly on the guitar.

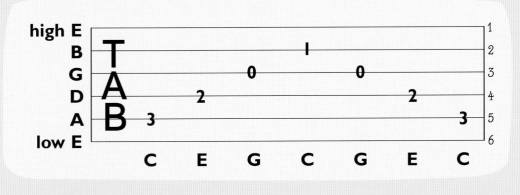

C E G C G E C

You will find lots of guitar music written in tablature, in books and on the internet. It is worth noting, however, that most tablature doesn't tell you about the lengths of the notes and the rhythm. It is also only read by guitarists, whereas traditional music symbols are read by singers and players of many different instruments.

Music and tab

On the next few pages in the book you will see the traditional music written above the tab, so you can see how both systems work.

This note is G.

This is how G is written in tablature.

This note is A.

This is how A is written in tablature.

Now see if you can play the following short exercises.

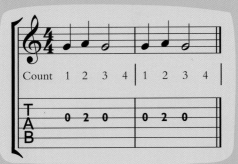

Count 1 2 3 4 | 1 2 3 4 |

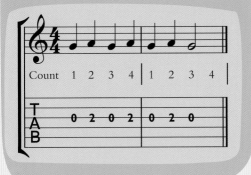

Count 1 2 3 4 | 1 2 3 4 |

Warm-up exercises

Try playing the following warm-up exercises. Play each exercise following the traditional music symbols first. You can cover up the tablature (tab) line, so that you follow the music on the staff.

Then play the exercises again reading the tab chart. The traditional music will help you learn the rhythm, while the tab will help you learn where to put your fingers. Both methods are useful to learn.

1.

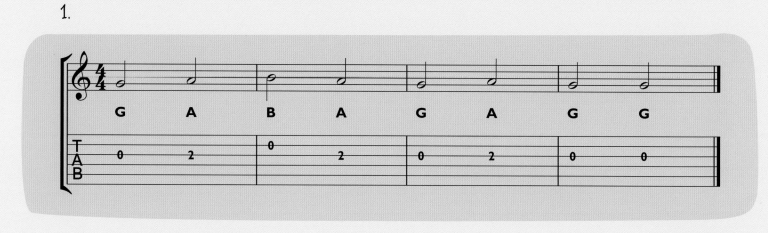

2.

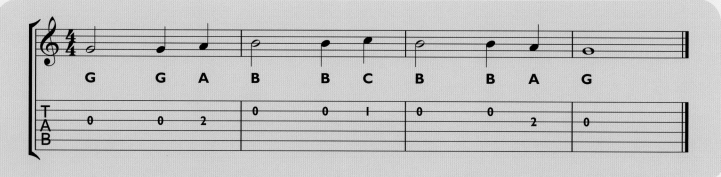

3.

Au clair de la lune

Now you are ready to learn how to play a melody. You only need to know three notes – G, A and B – to play this French folk tune. You can read the music on the staff, or follow the tab chart underneath. In the note diagrams, the string to play is marked in red.

When playing a new tune, it helps to clap the rhythm through first. Learn the notes and rhythm slowly, then gradually build up the speed.

Notes used

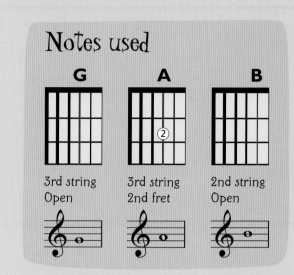

G — 3rd string Open
A — 3rd string 2nd fret
B — 2nd string Open

A time signature of 4/4 means there are four quarter note beats in every bar.

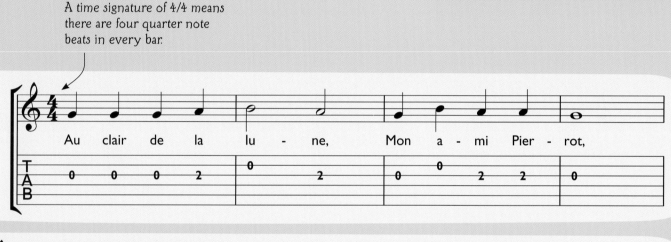

Au clair de la lu - ne, Mon a - mi Pier - rot,

Prêt - e moi ta plu - me, Pour é - crire un mot.

Sore fingers

After playing for a while, the fingers of your left hand may feel a little sore. But don't worry – after a couple of weeks, the skin on your fingertips will become tougher and your fingers will feel less tender.

What the words mean

Under the moonlight,
My friend Pierrot,
Lend me your pen,
So I can write a word.

Pease pudding hot

Earlier in this book there was a simple accompaniment to this song on three strings. Now you can learn to play the melody.

Look for the half note rests ▬ in the music. When you come to one, place your finger on the string you have just played to stop it from ringing, then rest for two beats.

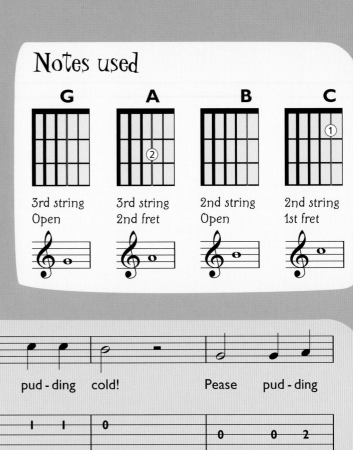

Notes used

G	A	B	C
3rd string Open	3rd string 2nd fret	2nd string Open	2nd string 1st fret

Rest for two beats. ⟶

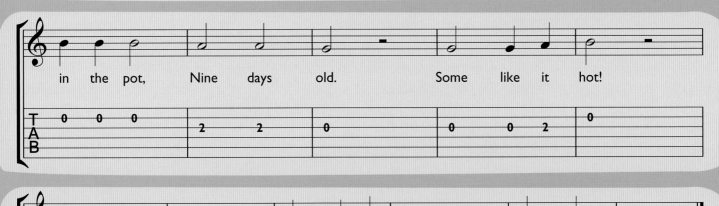

Pease pud-ding hot!   Pease pud-ding cold!   Pease pud-ding

in the pot,   Nine days old.   Some like it hot!

Some like it cold!   Some like it in the pot,   Nine days old.

Fretting fingers

Try not to let your fretting fingers move too far away from the fingerboard. If you move your fingers too much, you will not be able to play smoothly.

Tip

Try to keep alternating between your index and middle fingers when you pluck the strings.

I love little pussy

This song starts with two eighth notes on the 3rd beat of the bar. Before you begin, count "one, two," then start playing on the third beat. It helps to practice the following note sequence a few times: G A B C D C B A G.

Practice clapping the following rhythm before you start trying to learn the tune.

Fretting fingers

Remember to use different left-hand fingers to fret notes C, A and D. If you get used to the right fingers, you will find it easier when you want to play faster.

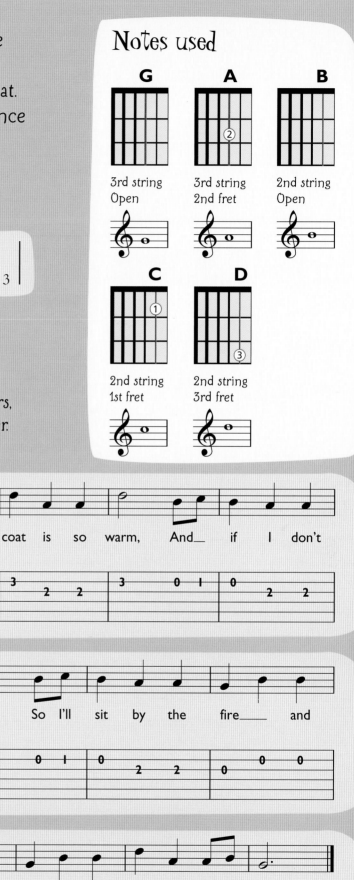

Notes used

G — 3rd string Open
A — 3rd string 2nd fret
B — 2nd string Open
C — 2nd string 1st fret
D — 2nd string 3rd fret

35

Yankee Doodle

There is one new note to learn in this song – F on the 1st string. To play it, press your 1st finger on the 1st string at the 1st fret.

Warm-up exercise

Before you start this tune, practice changing from C to D on the 2nd string. Keep your 1st finger on the 1st fret, and move your 3rd finger on and off the 3rd fret as you pluck the string. Practice this carefully until you can change smoothly from one note to the other.

This exercise will help strengthen the 3rd finger in your left hand, which is sometimes weak.

Notes used

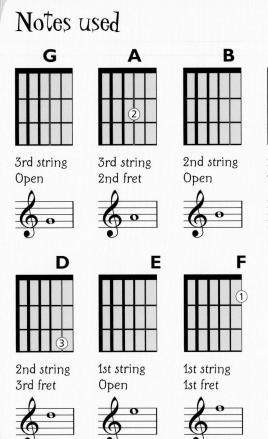

G — 3rd string Open
A — 3rd string 2nd fret
B — 2nd string Open
C — 2nd string 1st fret
D — 2nd string 3rd fret
E — 1st string Open
F — 1st string 1st fret

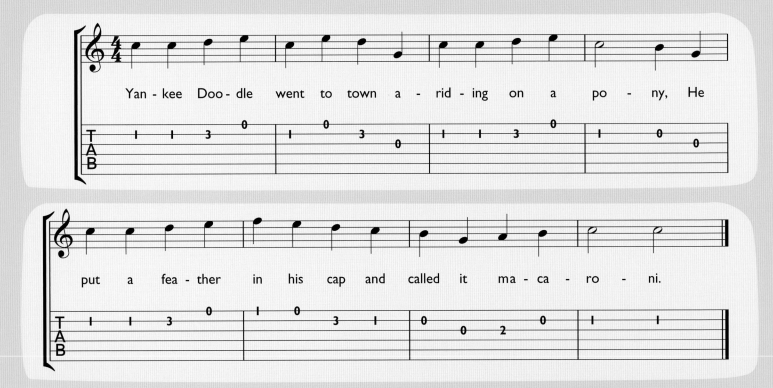

Yan - kee Doo - dle went to town a - rid - ing on a po - ny, He
put a fea - ther in his cap and called it ma - ca - ro - ni.

36

Pop! goes the weasel

This song has a time signature of 6/8. This means there are six eighth note beats in each bar. To get a feel for the rhythm, it helps to count "one, two, three, four, five, six," before you start the first bar.

Dotted quarter notes

This is a dotted quarter note. You can *see* some in the music below.

A dotted quarter note lasts for one and a half quarter notes, or three eighth notes.

Practice clapping this rhythm before you begin.

Tip

When you see a dotted quarter note in the music, count "one, two, three."

Notes used

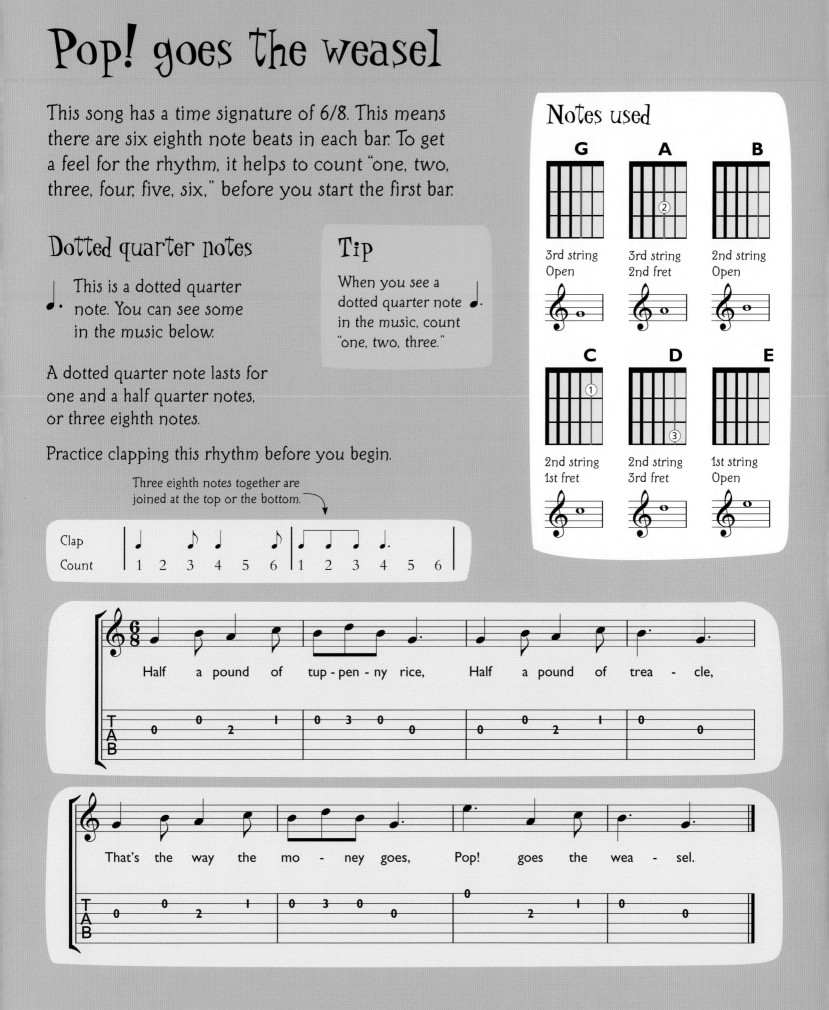

Hot cross buns

This song includes two groups of eight eighth notes that you will need to practice. Before learning the whole piece, play these notes (bars 5-6 and 13-14) three or four times, quite slowly at first, until you can play them smoothly.

This song includes the open bass string, D. You can pluck this note with your index finger or your thumb.

Quarter note rests

Look for the quarter note rests 𝄾 in the music.

When you come to one, touch the string with your finger to stop it from ringing, then rest for one beat.

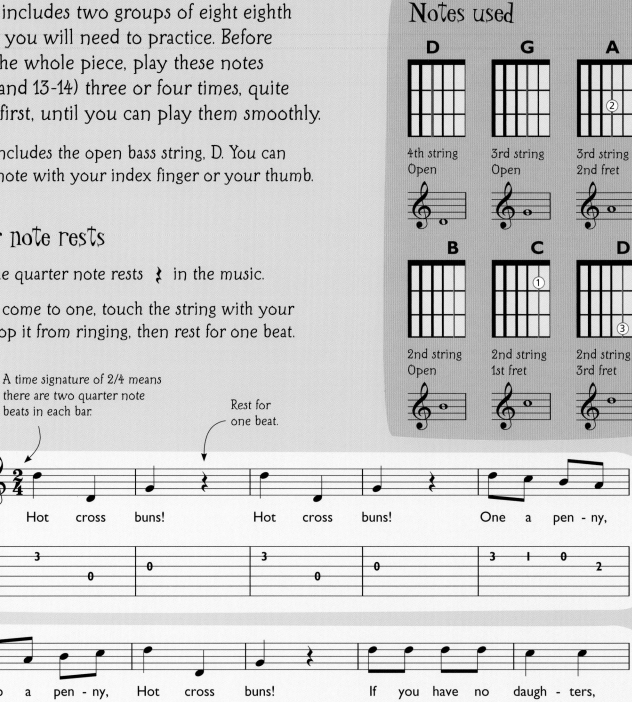

A time signature of 2/4 means there are two quarter note beats in each bar.

Rest for one beat.

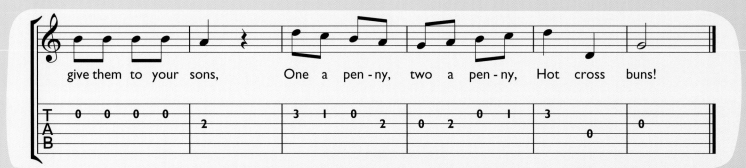

First chords

Playing chords

Chords are groups of notes played together. They are made by pressing the left-hand fingers onto the fingerboard, while the right hand plucks or strums the strings (see left). Chords are named after one of the notes in the group, usually the lowest bass note.

Strumming

Strumming is moving your thumb or a plectrum quickly across the strings so that they sound together. You can strum downward or upward.

Chord charts

Chord charts show you how to play different chords. The chart shows you where to place your left-hand fingers on the fingerboard, and which strings to play. The numbers in the circles show you which fingers to use.

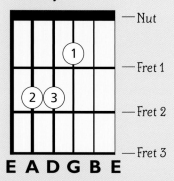

E major

E A D G B E

This is to remind you how the left-hand fingers are numbered.

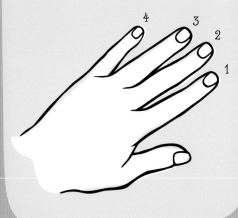

Fretting position

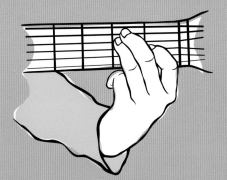

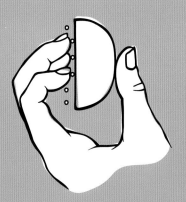

Press firmly on the fingerboard with your left-hand fingertips, just behind the frets, not on top of them. Keep your thumb low at the back of the neck.

Arch your fingers up over the strings. Make sure they don't touch any of the other strings otherwise the notes may not sound properly.

The downstrum

You can play a downstrum by strumming down across the strings toward the floor. Strum over the sound hole.

Thumb

Rest your thumb on the lowest string of the chord, then move it firmly downward across the strings. Try to make the strings sound at the same time.

Plectrum

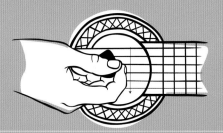

If you want to use a plectrum, hold it firmly between your thumb and index finger. Stroke firmly downward with the plectrum across the strings.

Three-string chords

There are lots of chords to learn on the guitar, but you can play many songs with just a few basic chords. The first chords you will learn are called "major" chords. In music, major chords are often known just by their letter name, for example, "E major" is known as "E." The following chords can be played by strumming just three strings.

Little C major

Place finger 1 of your left hand on the 2nd string at the 1st fret, as shown. Rest your right thumb on the 3rd string, over the sound hole, and play a downstrum.

An X above a string on the chord chart means you don't strum this string.

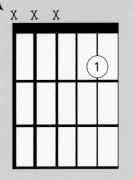

Little G major

Place finger 3 of your left hand on the 1st string at the 3rd fret, as shown. Starting from the 3rd string, strum downward toward the floor with your right thumb.

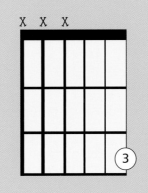

Strumming exercises

Most songs have a steady beat running through them. When playing chords, you need to feel this beat, and strum in time to it.

Try the following exercise, strumming once with a downstrum where you see this arrow ↓ .

1.
Strum Little C major (marked C below) to a beat of "one, two, three, four." Do this four times.

C	C	C	C
↓	↓	↓	↓
1	2	3	4

2.
Strum Little G major (marked G below) to a beat of "one, two, three, four." Do this four times.

G	G	G	G
↓	↓	↓	↓
1	2	3	4

3.
Now strum Little C for four beats followed by Little G for four beats. Do this many times until you can change chords quickly. Keep a steady beat as you play.

C	C	C	C
↓	↓	↓	↓
1	2	3	4
G	G	G	G
↓	↓	↓	↓
1	2	3	4

Go tell Aunt Nancy

In the following song, you will see the chord symbols, "C" and "G," above the melody and the words (lyrics). The chord symbols show you which chord to play in each bar and when to change from one to the other. The arrows show you when to strum.

Chords used

Little C
x x x
2nd string
1st fret

Little G
x x x
1st string
3rd fret

Strumming pattern

There are four beats in a bar. Play a downstrum on every other beat, like this:

Strum	↓		↓		↓		↓	
Count	1	2	3	4	1	2	3	4

Follow the chords, counting the beats as you play.

Where C is marked in the music, play Little C. Where G is marked, play Little G.

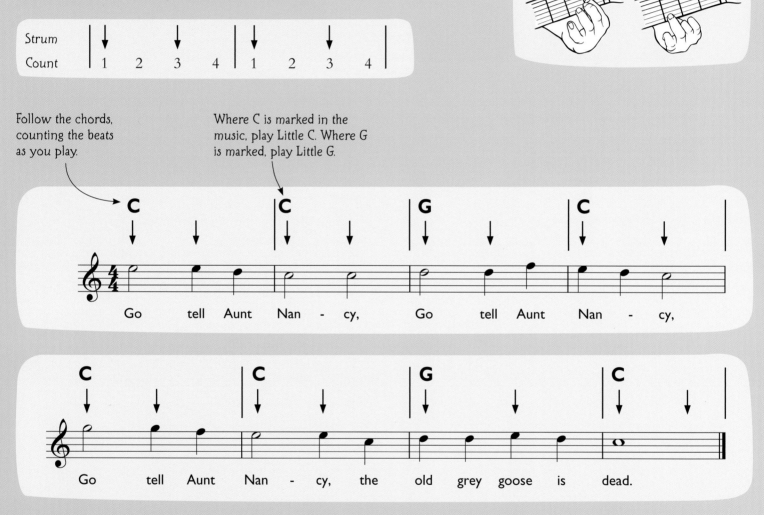

Go tell Aunt Nan - cy, Go tell Aunt Nan - cy,

Go tell Aunt Nan - cy, the old grey goose is dead.

Melody line

The music for the melody is included in this section, in case you want to learn the tune. It's also fun to play these songs as a duet. You could strum the chords, while another player plucks the tune, then switch.

If you are playing the melody, you need to recognize high G, at the top of the staff. To play this note, press your 3rd finger on the 1st string by the 3rd fret.

High G

Polly Wolly Doodle

Once you are used to the basic strumming movement, you can experiment with the way you play by making some strums sound stronger than others. In this song, try playing the first strum in every bar heavier than the rest.

Strumming pattern

There are four quarter note beats in a bar.
Play a downstrum on every beat, like this:

Strum	↓	↓	↓	↓	↓	↓	↓	↓
Count	1	2	3	4	1	2	3	4

Where C is marked in the music, play Little C. Where G is marked, play Little G.

Continue with this strumming pattern throughout the song.

Tip

Try to look ahead to see when a chord change is coming and get your fretting fingers ready.

Oh I went down south for to see my Sal, sing-ing Pol-ly Wol-ly Doo-dle all the

day, My__ Sal she is a spun-ky gal, sing-ing Pol-ly Wol-ly Doo-dle all the day!

Relaxed strumming hand

Keep your wrist loose and relaxed as you strum the chords to create a smooth flowing rhythm. Let the strumming movement come from your wrist, rather than your elbow. Your arm does not need to move very much.

Keeping a steady beat

Don't strum too quickly to start off with. It doesn't matter how slowly you play, as long as you keep strumming with a steady beat all the way through. When you change chords, try not to pause between strums.

Amazing grace

For this song, you need to learn a new chord called D7. You can strum this chord downward starting from the 4th string – D. Strum the first four strings for Little G too.

Chords used

D7
x x

Strum from the 4th string.

Little G
x x

Strum from the 4th string.

Little C
x x x

Strum from the 3rd string.

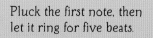

Strumming pattern

There are three beats in a bar. Strum on every beat, with a heavier strum on the first beat of each bar.

Strum	↓	↓	↓	↓	↓	↓	
Count	1	2	3	1	2	3	

Continue with this strumming pattern throughout the song.

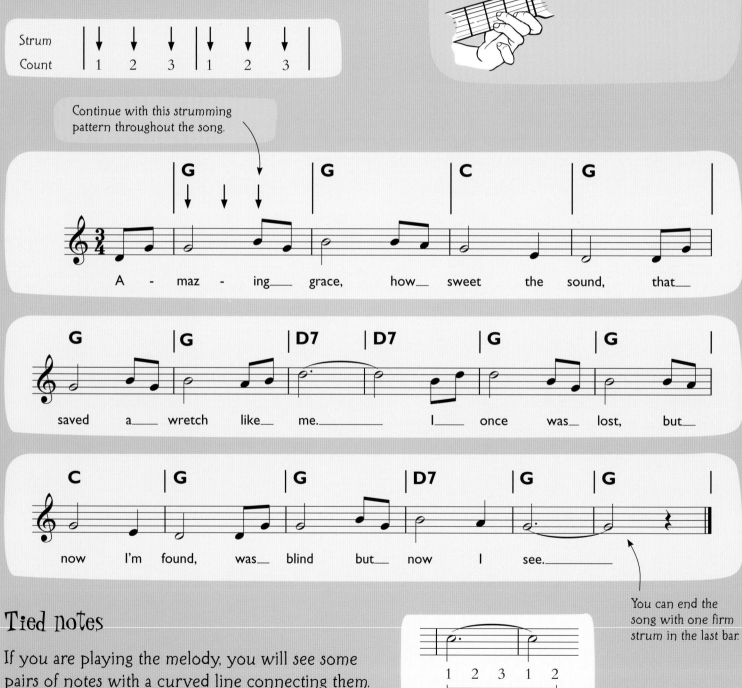

G   G   C   G

A - maz - ing— grace, how— sweet the sound, that—

G   G   D7   D7   G   G

saved a— wretch like— me.——— I once was— lost, but—

C   G   G   D7   G   G

now I'm found, was— blind but— now I see.———

You can end the song with one firm strum in the last bar.

Tied notes

If you are playing the melody, you will see some pairs of notes with a curved line connecting them. The curved line is called a tie. Play the first note, then let it ring for the value of both notes. You don't need to play the second note.

1 2 3 1 2

5 beats

Pluck the first note, then let it ring for five beats.

44

When the saints go marching in

Try playing the full chords of G major (G) and C major (C) in this song. Strum all six strings for G, and five strings for C. These chords are hard to do at first and will need lots of practice.

Strumming pattern

There are four beats in a bar. Strum on every beat, with a heavier strum on the first beat.

Strum	↓	↓	↓	↓	↓	↓	↓	↓
Count	1	2	3	4	1	2	3	4

Chords used

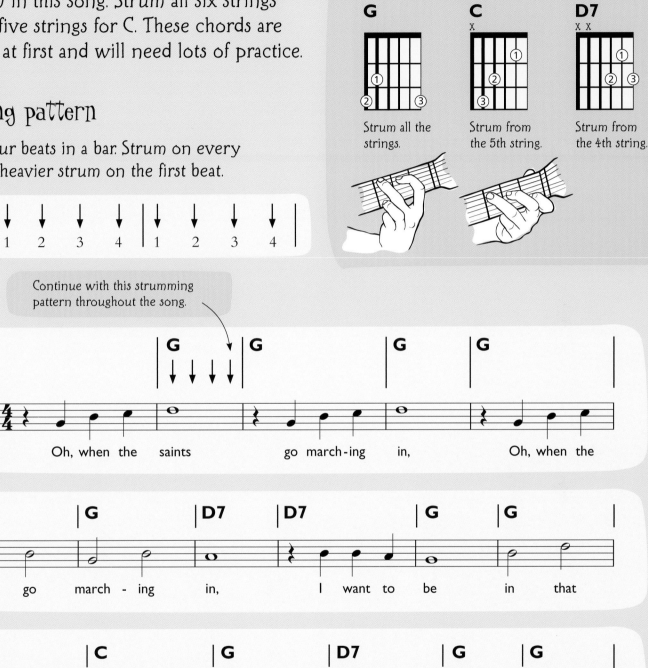

G — Strum all the strings.

C — Strum from the 5th string.

D7 — Strum from the 4th string.

Continue with this strumming pattern throughout the song.

Oh, when the saints go march-ing in, Oh, when the saints go march - ing in, I want to be in that num - ber,__ When the saints go march - ing in.

End the song with one firm strum in the last bar.

Tip

If the full chords of G and C are too difficult, you can play Little G and Little C instead.

Chord changes

If you find any of the chord changes hard to do, then try practicing them over and over again. You should try to change chords without looking at your fretting fingers.

45

Danny Boy

Here is another song you can play with the same three chords: G major, C major and D7.

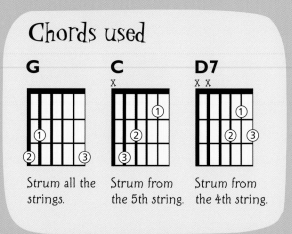

Chords used

G — Strum all the strings.

C — Strum from the 5th string.

D7 — Strum from the 4th string.

Strumming pattern

There are four beats in every bar. Strum the chords on every other beat, like this:

Strum	↓		↓		↓	↓		↓	
Count	1	2	3	4	1	2	3	4	

Key signature

G   G   C   C

Oh Dan-ny Boy,   the pipes, the pipes are call-ing,   From glen to

G   G   D7   D7   G   G

glen,   and down the moun-tain side,   The sum-mer's gone,   and   all the flow'rs are

C   C   G   D7   G   G

dy - ing,   'Tis you, 'tis you   must go and I must bide._____

End the song with one strum in the last bar.

Key signature

This is a sharp sign ♯. In the music there is a ♯ on the F line of every staff. This is called the key signature. It means that every F note is raised a semitone, and played one fret higher as F♯.

How to play F♯

To play the tune, you need to learn F♯ on the 4th string. To play it, press your 4th finger on the 4th string by the 4th fret. This may feel awkward, until you have built up strength in your 4th finger.

F♯

Joshua fought the battle of Jericho

Now you are ready to learn your first minor chords, E minor (Em) and A minor (Am). Before you start, practice changing chords from Am to Em then back to Am again.

Strumming pattern

There are four beats in a bar. Strum on every beat, with a firmer strum on the first beat of each bar.

Chords used

Notice that the Am and Em chord shapes are similar, which makes changing chords easier.

Em

Strum all the strings.

Am

Strum from the 5th string.

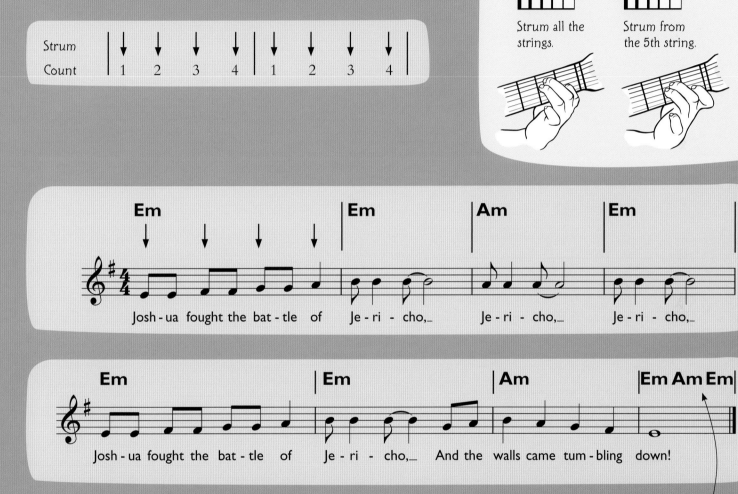

You can just play Em in the last bar until you are ready to play three fast chord changes from Em to Am to Em.

Fast chord changes

When switching from Em to Am, just shift the 2nd and 3rd fingers down a string and place your 1st finger on the 2nd string, by the 1st fret. The smaller the movements in your left hand between chords, the faster and smoother your chord changes will be.

47

Michael, row the boat ashore

In this song you need to learn the chords of D major (D) and A major (A). You can make your strumming sound more interesting and rhythmical by mixing downstrums and upstrums together.

The upstrum

Rest your thumb beneath the 1st string and strum upward toward your face. The upstrum should sound weaker than the downstrum.

An upstrum is marked with a ↑ .

Strumming pattern

Alternate your strumming between downstrums and upstrums. Let the downstrums fall in time with each quarter note beat. Practice this now with D major.

Strum	↓ ↑ ↓ ↑ ↓ ↑ ↓ ↑	↓ ↑ ↓ ↑ ↓ ↑ ↓ ↑
Count	1 and 2 and 3 and 4 and	1 and 2 and 3 and 4 and

Chords used

D
X X

Don't strum the 5th and 6th strings.

A
X

Don't strum the 6th string.

G

Strum all the strings for a downstrum.

Relaxed wrist

As you alternate between downstrums and upstrums, just move your wrist, and not your whole arm. To do this fast, you need to keep your wrist loose and relaxed.

Continue this strumming pattern throughout the song.

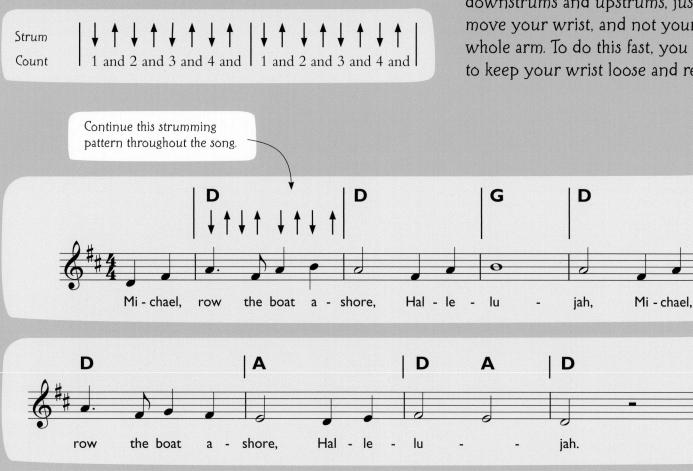

D   D   G   D

Mi - chael, row the boat a - shore, Hal - le - lu - jah, Mi - chael,

D |A |D A |D |

row the boat a - shore, Hal - le - lu - jah.

Oh! Susanna

To play this song, you need to learn A7. There are four quarter note beats in each bar. As you strum, make sure the downstrums fall on the beat, while the upstrums fall between the beats.

Chords used

D
x x

Don't strum the 5th and 6th strings.

G

Strum all the strings for a downstrum.

A7
x

Don't strum the 6th string.

Strumming pattern

Use a similar pattern to the last song, alternating your strumming between downstrums and upstrums.

Strum | ↓ ↑ ↓ ↑ ↓ ↑ ↓ ↑ | ↓ ↑ ↓ ↑ ↓ ↑ ↓ ↑
Count | 1 and 2 and 3 and 4 and | 1 and 2 and 3 and 4 and

Continue with this strumming pattern throughout the song.

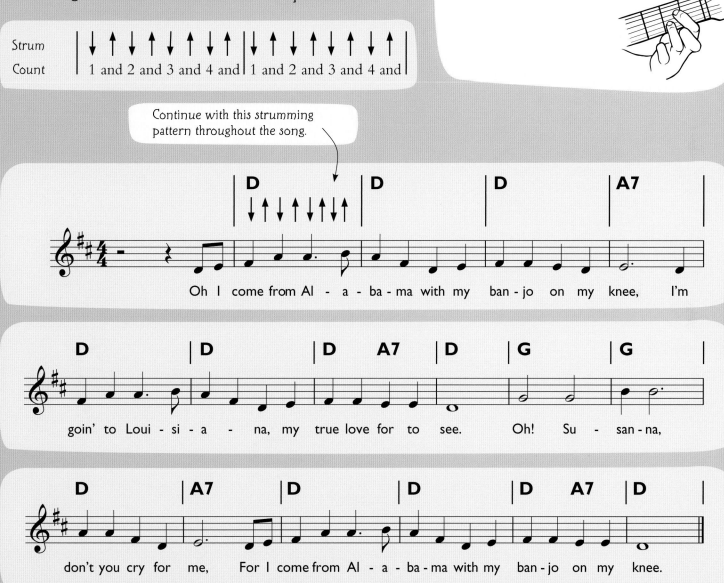

Oh I come from Al - a - ba - ma with my ban - jo on my knee, I'm

goin' to Loui - si - a - na, my true love for to see. Oh! Su - san - na,

don't you cry for me, For I come from Al - a - ba - ma with my ban - jo on my knee.

Strumming fewer strings

You don't have to strum all the strings when playing an upstrum. You can experiment by just strumming the first three or four strings.

She'll be coming round the mountain

This song uses the chords of D and A. Practice switching between these two chords, then try using the new strumming pattern below.

Chords used

D
X X

Don't strum the 5th and 6th strings.

A
X

Don't strum the 6th string.

Strumming pattern

Strum with a firm downward stroke on the 1st beat, followed by alternating downstrums and upstrums on the 2nd, 3rd and 4th beats, like this:

Strum	↓ ↓ ↑ ↓ ↑ ↓ ↑	↓ ↓ ↑ ↓ ↑ ↓ ↑
Count	1　2 and 3 and 4 and	1　2 and 3 and 4 and

Rhythm	♩ ♫ ♫
Count	1　2 and 3 and 4 and

Continue with this strumming pattern throughout the song.

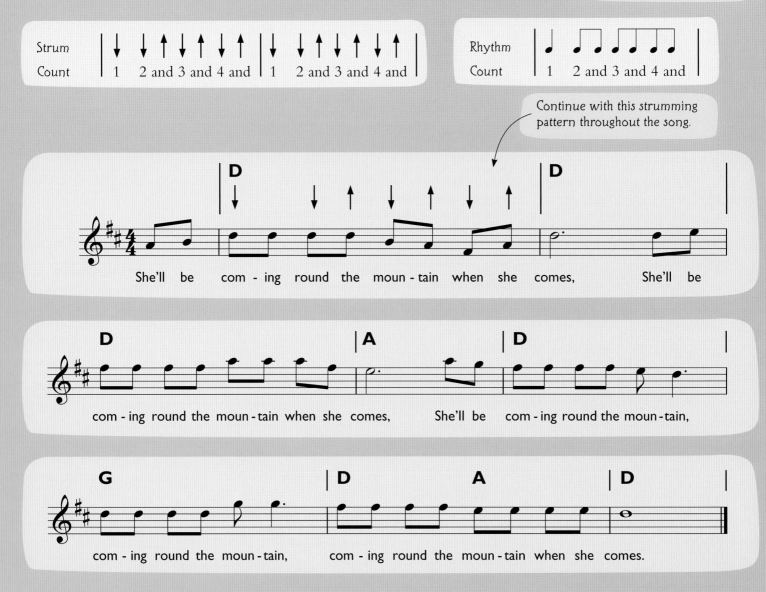

She'll be com-ing round the moun-tain when she comes, She'll be

com-ing round the moun-tain when she comes, She'll be com-ing round the moun-tain,

com-ing round the moun-tain, com-ing round the moun-tain when she comes.

New notes

If you are playing the melody, you need to learn F♯ and high A. To play F♯, press your 2nd finger on the 1st string by the 2nd fret. To play high A, press your 4th finger on the 1st string by the 5th fret.

F♯

high A

High A sits on its own little line above the staff, called a leger line.

What shall we do with the drunken sailor?

This song uses the chords of Em and D. Practice switching between these two chords, then play this song with a similar strumming pattern to the previous song.

Chords used

Em

Strum all the strings.

D
x x

Don't strum the 5th and 6th strings.

Strumming pattern

This song has four beats in a bar. Strum with a downstrum on the 1st beat, followed by alternating downstrums and upstrums.

Strum	↓	↓ ↑ ↓ ↑ ↓ ↑	↓	↓ ↑ ↓ ↑ ↓ ↑
Count	1	2 and 3 and 4 and	1	2 and 3 and 4 and

New note

If you are playing the melody, look for C♯ played on the 2nd string by the 2nd fret.

C♯

Em ↓ ↓ ↑ ↓ ↑ ↓ ↑   **Em**   **D**

What shall we do with the drunk - en sai - lor? What shall we do with the

D   **Em**   **Em**   **D**

drunk - en sai - lor? What shall we do with the drunk - en sai - lor? Ear - ly in the

Em   **Em**   **Em**   **D**   **D**

mor - ning! Hoo - ray and up she ris - es, Hoo - ray and up she ri - ses,

Em   **Em**   **D**   **Em**

Hoo - ray and up she ris - es, Ear - ly in the mor - ning!

The animals went in two by two

In this song you will learn a new chord, E7. Strum the chord through slowly, making sure that all the notes ring clearly.

Chords used

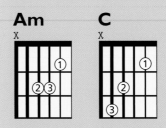

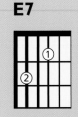

Am — Don't strum the 6th string.

C — Don't strum the 6th string.

Em — Strum all the strings for a downstrum.

E7 — Strum all the strings for a downstrum.

Strumming pattern

This song has six eighth note beats in each bar. You can try this strumming pattern with an upstrum on the last beat of the bar.

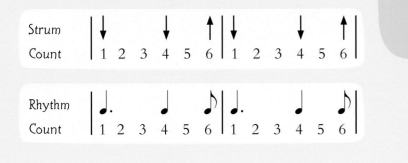

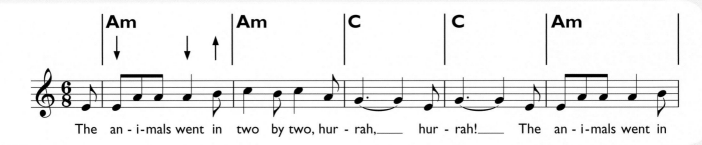

Tied notes

If you are playing the melody, play the tied notes in the music for five eighth note beats.

To begin with, play only the Am chord in the last two bars. When you are ready, try the fast chord change, from Am to E7 to Am again.

Finger-picking

Right-hand fingering

Finger-picking creates a more gentle, lighter alternative to strumming and is common in folk, classical and jazz music. With finger-picking, it's important to use the correct fingers for each string. The right-hand fingers have special names in guitar music. They are known by the letters "p, i, m, a." This comes from the Spanish names for each finger.

p   stands for pulgar, which means "thumb."
i   stands for indicio, which means "index finger."
m   stands for medio, which means "middle finger."
a   stands for anular, which means "ring finger."

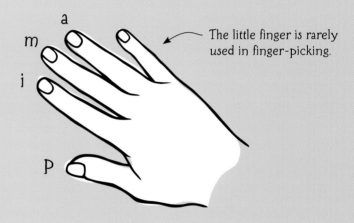

The little finger is rarely used in finger-picking.

P i m a fingers and strings

Where you see "p i m a" above the notes in this book:

p, the thumb, plucks the main bass string of the chord;
i, the index finger, always plucks the 3rd string;
m, the middle finger, always plucks the 2nd string;
a, the ring finger, always plucks the 1st string.

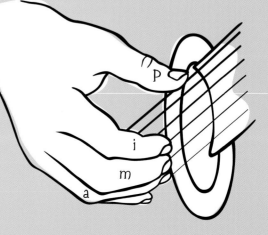

Pluck out from the treble strings, using a grabbing motion. Let your fingers end the stroke above the strings.

Finger-picking exercises

There are lots of different finger-picking patterns you can try. The following exercises show three different styles.

Try these exercises using the correct "p i m a" fingers.

In each exercise, you need to pluck the open strings, low E, G, B and high E.

Play each exercise four times.

1.

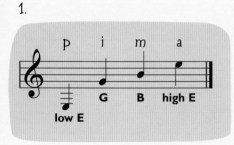

2.

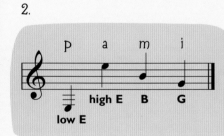

3.

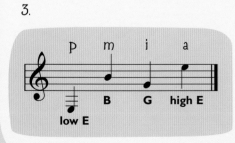

What shall we do with the drunken sailor?

Now you should be ready to learn how to play this song in a finger-picking style. Use your thumb (p) to pluck the main bass note for each chord. For E minor it plucks the 6th string, while for D major, it plucks the 4th string.

Finger-picking pattern

Pluck with your thumb (p), followed by your index finger (i), your middle finger (m) and your ring finger (a), like this:

Pluck	p	i	m	a	p	i	m	a
Count	1	2	3	4	1	2	3	4

Chords used

Your thumb switches between plucking the 6th and the 4th string, while your "ima" fingers pluck the three treble strings.

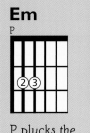
Em
P plucks the 6th string.

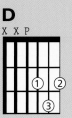
D
P plucks the 4th string.

Donkey riding

For this accompaniment, use the same finger-picking pattern, "p i m a," that you used in the last song. Your thumb (p) plucks the 4th string for D major, the 5th string for A major and the 6th string for G major.

Chords used

Your thumb switches between plucking the 4th, 5th and the 6th strings for these chords. The "ima" fingers pluck the treble strings.

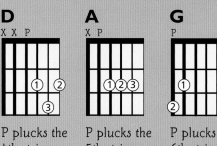

D	A	G
X X P	X P	P
P plucks the 4th string.	P plucks the 5th string.	P plucks the 6th string.

Finger-picking pattern

Pluck with your thumb (p) followed by your index finger (i), your middle finger (m) and your ring finger (a), like this:

Pluck	p	i	m	a	p	i	m	a
Count	1	2	3	4	1	2	3	4

D **D** **A** **A**

p i m a

Were you e-ver in Que-bec? Stow-ing tim-ber__ on the deck?

D **D** **A** **D**

See the king with the gold-en crown, Rid-ing on a don-key.

Pluck only the bass strings in this section. — Continue plucking p i m a.

G D **A D** **A** **A**

P P P P p i m a p i m a

Hey__ ho and a-way we go, Don-key rid-ing, don-key rid-ing,

Pluck only the bass strings in this section. — Continue plucking p i m a.

G D **A D** **A** **D**

P P P P p i m a p i m a

Hey__ ho and a-way we go, Rid-ing on a don-key!

Molly Malone

This song has three beats in a bar, so it has a slightly different finger-picking rhythm. Your thumb (p) plucks the 4th string for D major and the 5th string for A major.

Finger-picking pattern

Pluck "p i m a m i" over two bars. Try it now for the chords of D major and A major. Practice switching from D major to A major and back to D major again.

Pluck	p	i	m	a	m	i
Count	1	2	3	1	2	3

Chords used

Your thumb alternates between the 4th and 5th strings in this song.

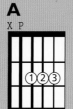

P plucks the 4th string.

P plucks the 5th string.

Think about where your thumb is moving to before each chord change.

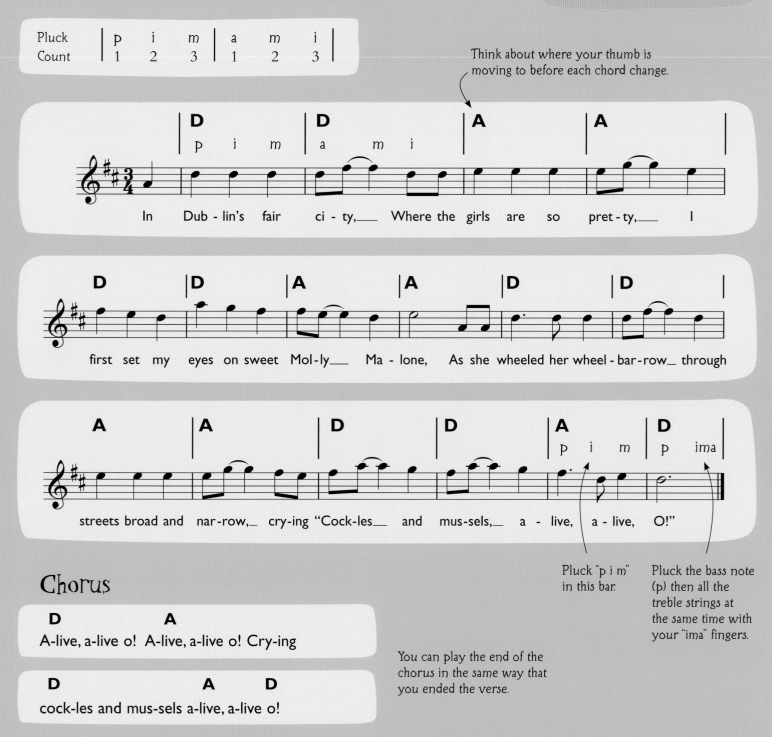

In Dub-lin's fair ci-ty,___ Where the girls are so pret-ty,___ I

first set my eyes on sweet Mol-ly___ Ma - lone, As she wheeled her wheel-bar-row_ through

streets broad and nar-row,_ cry-ing "Cock-les___ and mus-sels,_ a - live, a - live, O!"

Pluck "p i m" in this bar.

Pluck the bass note (p) then all the treble strings at the same time with your "ima" fingers.

Chorus

D	A

A-live, a-live o! A-live, a-live o! Cry-ing

D	A	D

cock-les and mus-sels a-live, a-live o!

You can play the end of the chorus in the same way that you ended the verse.

House of the Rising Sun

In this song you need to learn two chords – E major (E) and F major (F). F is the hardest chord you have learned so far, because to play it, you need to fret two strings with one finger. This technique is called barre.

Finger-picking pattern

This accompaniment uses a similar pattern to the previous song, but has six beats in each bar, instead of three. Pluck "p i m a m i" in each bar. Practice this now in the chord of A minor.

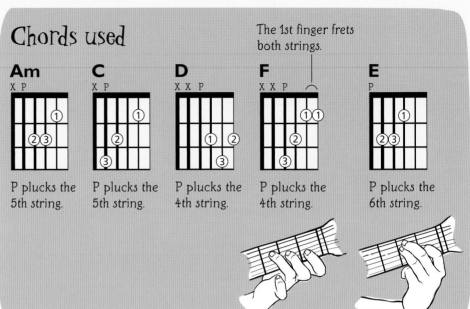

Chords used

The 1st finger frets both strings.

Am	C	D	F	E
X P	X P	X X P	X X P	P

P plucks the 5th string. — P plucks the 5th string. — P plucks the 4th string. — P plucks the 4th string. — P plucks the 6th string.

Pluck	p i m a m i	p i m a m i
Count	1 2 3 4 5 6	1 2 3 4 5 6

Tip

You will need to practice playing the F chord over and over again until you can make all the notes ring clearly.

There is____ a house___ in New Or - leans,___ They call____ the Ris - ing___

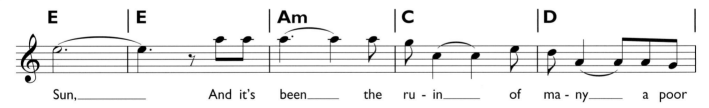

Sun,_____ And it's been____ the ru - in_____ of ma - ny____ a poor

boy,_____ and me,_____ I know____ I'm one.____

* To play this G♯ , press your 1st finger on the 3rd string by the 1st fret.

Helpful information

Tuning - the 5th fret trick

The 5th fret trick is a quick way of tuning the guitar to itself. Once you know how to do it, you will be able to make your guitar sound in tune wherever you are.

Ideally, you need to tune the 6th string using a tuner, (see page 10). Then, use the 5th fret trick to tune the remaining strings. If you don't have a tuner, assume the 6th string is in tune.

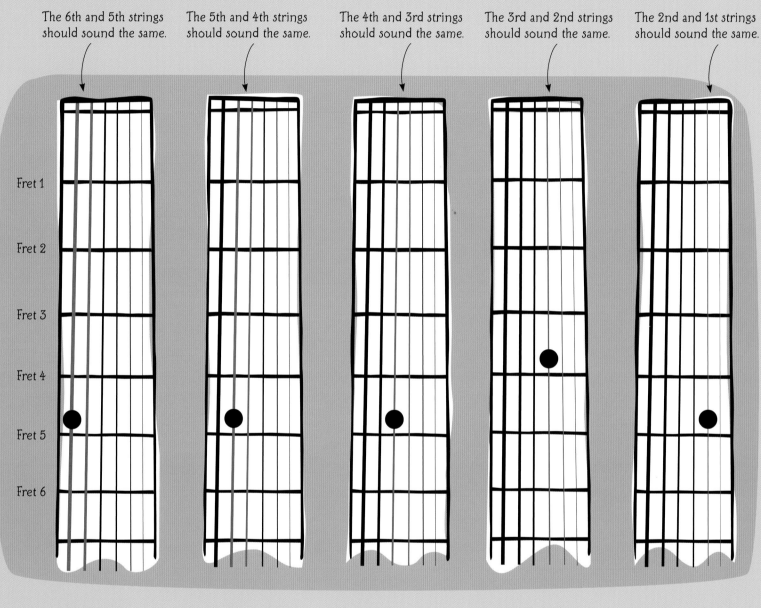

The 6th and 5th strings should sound the same.

The 5th and 4th strings should sound the same.

The 4th and 3rd strings should sound the same.

The 3rd and 2nd strings should sound the same.

The 2nd and 1st strings should sound the same.

Fret 1
Fret 2
Fret 3
Fret 4
Fret 5
Fret 6

1. Press the 6th string by the 5th fret. Play this note, then the open 5th string. Tighten or loosen the 5th string until both strings sound the same.

2. Press the 5th string by the 5th fret. Play this note, then play the open 4th string. Tune the 4th string until both strings sound the same.

3. Press the 4th string by the fifth fret. Play this note, then the open 3rd string. Adjust the 3rd string until both strings sound the same.

4. Press the 3rd string by the 4th fret. Play this note, then the open 2nd string. Tune the 2nd string until both strings sound the same.

5. Press the 2nd string by the 5th fret. Play this note and the open 1st string. Tighten or loosen the 1st string until both strings sound the same.

Afterwards, you can slowly strum through the chord of E major, to help you check that all the notes sound in tune.

Restringing your guitar

After several months of playing your guitar, the strings may start to sound dull and become harder to tune. When this happens, it's time to restring your guitar. You may also need to replace a string if one snaps.

To remove an old string, unwind the tuning peg until the string comes loose, then untie the string at the bridge end and pull it out. When buying new strings, make sure you buy the right kind of strings for your guitar.

Classical guitars

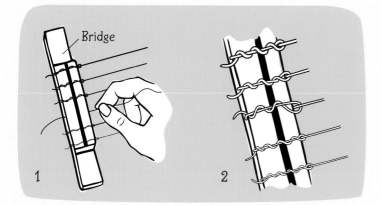

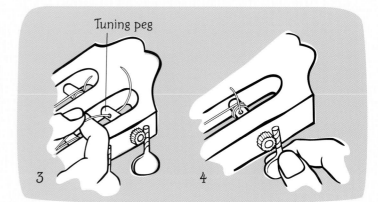

Thread the end of the string through the bridge from the sound hole side, leaving about 8cm (3in) sticking out from the end. Loop this end under the string where it enters the bridge, then twist it around itself two or three times to attach it. Pull the string quite firmly to help secure it at the bridge.

Thread the other end of the string across the nut and through a hole in the tuning peg, leaving about 2cm (3/4in) sticking out. Turn the tuning peg counterclockwise with one hand, while pulling the string taught with the other. Keep winding carefully until the string is fairly tight, then tune it.

Steel string and electric guitars

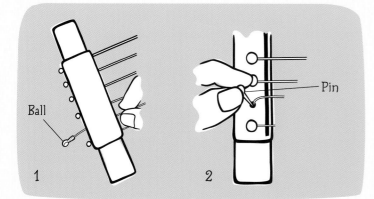

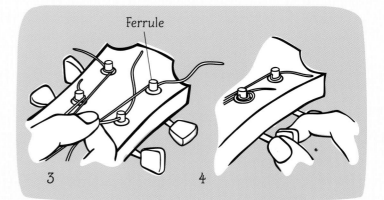

Electric and steel strings have a ball at the end which helps to secure the string. Thread the string through the bridge toward the sound hole and pull it through. If there is a pin, remove it from its hole and place the ball inside the hole. Then, insert the pin into the hole, making sure it is secure.

Pull the string up to the neck. Thread the string through a hole in the ferrule, leaving the string fairly slack between the bridge and the neck. Tighten the string by turning the tuning peg, until the string is fairly taught. Then, tune the string. You can use wire cutters to cut off any excess string.

Chord charts

On this page you can see how to play all the chords used in this book. In each chord chart, the nut is at the top, the vertical lines represent the strings, while the horizontal lines represent the frets.

The circles show you where to put your fretting fingers and the numbers in the circles show you which fretting finger to use. An X above the string tells you not to play that string.

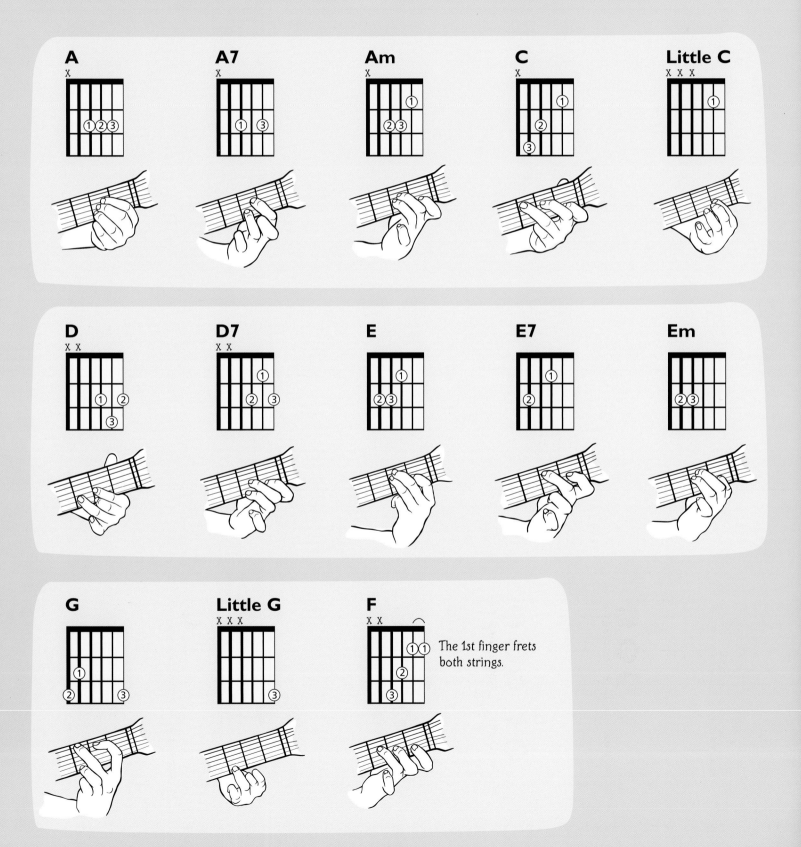

The 1st finger frets both strings.

Reading notes in music

This diagram shows you where all the notes used in this book appear on the staff and in tablature (tab). In tab, the top line is the 1st string – high E. The symbol "0" means the string is open – you don't fret the string – a "1" means fret the 1st fret, and so on.

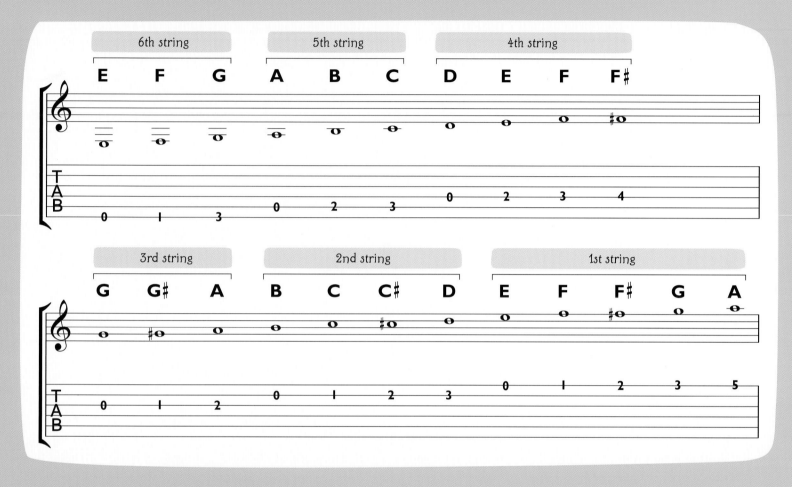

Finding notes on the guitar

The diagram below shows you how to play all the notes used in this book, up to a high A on the 1st string. On the left side are the note names for each open string. The circles show you where to place your fretting fingers. The note names are written inside the circles.

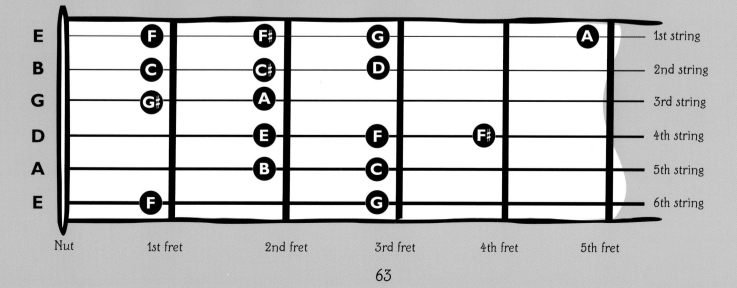

List of songs

Index

This edition published in 2009 by Usborne Publishing Ltd. Usborne House, 83–85 Saffron Hill, London ECIN 8RT, England. www.usborne.com
Copyright © 2009 Usborne Publishing Ltd. The name Usborne and the devices ♀ ⊕ are Trade Marks of Usborne Publishing Ltd.